DISCOVERING GOD'S CHURCH:

WHERE GOD IS CALLING DISCIPLES TO GATHER TO SERVE HIM

WRITTEN BY KEITH DORRICOTT

(BOOK TWO OF "ARE WE MISSING SOMETHING?")

"the church of God which He purchased with His own blood" (Acts 20:28)

CHAPTER ONE: WHAT IS A CHURCH?

"When you come together as a church ..." (1 Corinthians 11:18)

When people talk about a church these days they are commonly referring to a religious building, a place of worship. We may be encouraged to "worship at a church near you," or talk about "going to church" or constructing a new church. In fact the buildings themselves often have signs labelling them as churches. But this is not the Bible meaning of the word.

Ekklesia

The Bible word for church, *"ekklesia,"* meaning people called out to be together, is used in several contexts. We have already looked at its use in connection with "the church the Body of Christ". Israel in the wilderness is referred to in Acts 7:38 as *"the church in the wilderness"* (translated as "church" in the King James Version, "assembly" in the NIV, and "congregation" in the NKJV and NASB). It is also used for secular gatherings (e.g. Acts 19:39). But the most common usage is of local gatherings of God's people, where the term "church of God" is used, to denote that it is God who has called them together. This is the only use in the New Testament in which the word occurs both in the singular (e.g. 1 Corinthians 1:2) and the plural (e.g. 1 Corinthians 11:16). Each church of God was identified with a particular place, such as Jerusalem (Galatians 1:13), Corinth (1 Corinthians 1:2), and Thessalonica (1 Thessalonians 1:1). In Jerusalem, on the Day of Pentecost, the disciples who were baptized and added to the approximately one hundred and twenty who were already gathered together had been called together by God, as "the church of God" in that place.

Why Does Church Matter?

There is certainly no shortage of Christian church groups and denominations to choose from these days. A believer in many countries who wishes to gather with other believers can find an almost unlimited variety. Is this a good thing? It certainly caters to various preferences, cultures, and traditions. People are free to choose as they like on the basis of convenience of location, ethnic background, the pastor, the programs that are offered, where friends and family members attend, and so on. There is a widespread view that the actual basis on which Christians gather together is not that important since, after all, they are all members of that one "true church," which is Christ's Body.

Some believers may say that it is not that important whether a Christian belongs to a church or not. If, as some say, the essence of the Christian faith is the personal relationship between a believer and Jesus Christ, then any church affiliation is secondary; it is there primarily as an option to support their personal Christian walk. Thus, they would argue, Christians should feel free to come and go as they please. But is this in fact what the Scriptures teach, or are we again missing something?

We do not have to study our Bibles for very long before we realize that living out our Christian lives necessarily includes our relationships with other believers. For example, while the well-known verse John 3:16 tells us about how we obtain salvation, a corresponding verse in 1 John chapter 3 links that with the importance of our relationship with each other: *"This is His commandment: that we believe in the name of His Son Jesus Christ and love one another, as He commanded us"* (1 John 3:23).

Loving one another is one of the foremost commands to the Christian. Jesus said that this was how other people would know that they were His disciples (John 13:35). We cannot fulfill that command by staying apart from other Christians or by picking and choosing those whom we will gather with just to suit ourselves.

What Should the Church Be Called?

Today churches are called by various names, perhaps reflecting their denominational association, community location, or some other characteristic. Sometimes contests are held to find a name for a new church. However, what matters is not what we may choose to call it but what God calls it. If "*ekklesia*" refers to the fact that God has called disciples together into His churches, then it is God who must put His name on them, just as He put His name on His people Israel in Old Testament times. (He also put His name on the city of Jerusalem: *"Jerusalem, the city where I have chosen for Myself to put My name"* (1 Kings 11:36). That is what made it the holy city, the city of God.)

For this reason the name that was given to local churches in the New Testament was "church of God." Each was God's church; otherwise, it would have had no right to take that name for itself.

God puts His name on something only when it belongs to Him and meets His requirements. Various other expressions using the word "church" occur in various places:

- The church in a house (e.g. Romans 16:5; 1 Corinthians 16:19; Colossians 4:15), referring to one or more homes where the saints in the church of God in the town met.
- "*The church of the living God*" (1 Timothy 3:15), referring to the house of God, as discussed in the last section.
- "*The church throughout all Judea and Galilee and Samaria*" (Acts 9:31), referring to the aggregate of all those in the churches of God in those regions.
- "*The churches of the saints*" (1 Corinthians 14:33), emphasizing that it is saints who make up the churches.
- "*The churches of Christ*" (Romans 16:16), also referring to local gatherings of those in churches of God, emphasizing the character and authority of Christ over them (as seen in Revelation 1:12,13).

God Calls Us To Church

When the apostle Paul came for the first time to the city of Corinth in Achaia he had a lot of opposition. He was tempted to leave and go elsewhere, but the Lord told him to stay because "*I have many people in this city*" (Acts 18:10). Because of his work there, "*the church of God which is at Corinth*" came into existence (1 Corinthians 1:2; 2 Corinthians 2:1). It was established by disciples responding in obedience to the call of God. This was the same basis as every other church of God had been and would be in the future. That was the church to which he wrote his two epistles.

Different Callings

In his first epistle, Paul used the word "call" four times in the first nine verses, and each time it had a somewhat different meaning. Firstly, he mentioned his own individual *calling* to be an apostle: *"Paul, called as an apostle of Jesus Christ"* (verse 1). This referred to God having summoned him to his particular ministry, as described in Acts 13:2,3, although He had predetermined it from eternity (Acts 13:2,3; Galatians 1:15; 2 Timothy 1:8,9).

Secondly, he told the church that God had *called* them to be saints (that is, His holy ones): *"To the church of God which is at Corinth, to those who have been sanctified in Christ Jesus, saints by calling"* (verse 2). The word "saints" is always used in this collective sense in the New Testament; we never read of an individual saint.

Thirdly, he mentioned that they were linked with saints in other places, *"with all who in every place call on the name of our Lord Jesus Christ, their Lord and ours"* (verses 2,3). This expression "call on the name of the Lord" is referring to their spiritual activity, and occurs throughout Scripture, beginning in Genesis 4:26. It is used to refer to those in the churches of God whom Paul himself persecuted (Acts 9:21), and was the hallmark of those gathered in churches of God.

Finally, he told them that God had *"called"* them into a fellowship: *"God is faithful, by whom you were called into the fellowship of His Son, Jesus Christ our Lord"* (verse 9 NKJV). The Greek work for *call,* meaning "to summon," is the same word as the one used to call someone by their own name. In effect, God had called them out by name. It was a personal calling.

Note that in verse 9 it is *"the fellowship of,"* not "fellowship with," as some translations put it. It was not referring to their individual fellowship *"with"* Jesus Christ (1 John 1:6), but to a defined community of disciples. This is as it was with the original church in Jerusalem; they *"continued steadfastly in ... the fellowship ..."* (Acts 2:42). Therefore, these saints in Corinth had been called into the same fellowship as those in the churches of God elsewhere. God was faithful; He had committed Himself to them, and He expected them in turn to commit themselves to Him (and to each other). It was a partnership, a community, of separated believers which belonged to the Lord Jesus.

As followers of the Lord Jesus, we can see that the choice of church gathering is not really up to us. Since it is God who calls disciples together for divine activity, we should look for and respond to His call. Casual fellowship, shopping around (or hopping around) from one church to another, is not the scriptural way. It is the people who form the church. Disciples are therefore expected to belong to it, to "be" the church, to commit themselves to it and not to leave it (except to move to another such church of God). If God calls us into it, He will not later call us out of it (Romans 11:29).

This is a very different concept of church than is prevalent in the world today. But Scripture shows us that it is the Lord's way, as is evident from the first church that was brought into existence in Jerusalem almost two thousand years ago, which we will look at now.

CHAPTER TWO: THE FIRST CHURCH OF GOD

"A great persecution began against the church in Jerusalem." (Acts 8:1)

"I persecuted the church of God." (1 Corinthians 15:9)

The churches of God that were established in New Testament times serve as the model for us today. The early chapters of the book of Acts are far more than just a historical account of what happened in those days; they serve as a pattern for us to follow. While some things were undoubtedly only relevant to those times, what is recorded for us in Scripture generally applies for us to practice today, even though we live centuries later.

The first century model is applicable to the twenty-first century. The first church of God was in Jerusalem, the very city in which the Lord Jesus had been crucified and buried. It had been the destination of the earthly people of God in the Old Testament, and it became the starting point for the people of God in New Testament times. Because it was the first church and set the pattern, it is particularly instructive. This is often the case; the first occurrence of something in Scripture generally sets a pattern for what follows, which is why the book of Genesis is often called "the seed-plot of the Bible."

The Church in Jerusalem

Let's examine this church of God in Jerusalem. It came into existence on the day of Pentecost about ten days after the Lord Jesus had returned to heaven. He had spent the time between His resurrection and His final departure instructing His apostles: *"... appearing to them over a period of forty days and speaking of the things concerning the kingdom of God"* (Acts 1:3). We are not told the details of what He said to them, but we can infer it very clearly from the Acts of the Apostles and the epistles.

Towards the end of that period, the Lord gave them what is often referred to as the Great Commission: *"Go therefore and make disciples of all the nations, baptizing them in the name of the Father and the Son and the Holy Spirit, teaching them to observe all that I commanded you; and lo, I am with you always, even to the end of the age"* (Matthew 28:19,20). He told them to wait in Jerusalem until they received *"power from on high"* (Luke 24:49), referring to the Holy Spirit. When Pentecost came, *"they were all together in one place"* (Acts 2:1), and the Spirit was poured out on them. Then they began to carry out exactly what the Lord had told them to do.

A crowd gathered. Peter stood up and preached to them. About three thousand people responded in faith to his preaching. They were then immediately baptized in water and were added to those one hundred and twenty (or so) disciples who were already together (Acts 1:15). And they continued from then on with them: *"So then, those who had received his word were baptized;*

and that day there were added about three thousand souls. They were continually devoting themselves to the apostles' teaching and to fellowship, to the breaking of bread and to prayer" (Acts 2:41,42).

This is how the church of God in Jerusalem came into existence. One by one disciples were made, were baptized by immersion, and were added to their number. Even though three thousand of them were added on that one day, they were individually added to what had been the smaller group that already existed. This was not a group merger.

Being Added to the Lord

We are told that, as disciples were being added to the church, the Lord was adding them to Himself. It says they were *"added to the Lord"* (Acts 5:14 NKJV). And so we are introduced to the position of being *"in the Lord"* (Greek: *en kurioo*), which occurs frequently in the epistles. This is a distinct term, different from our position of being "in Christ" or "in Christ Jesus," such as, *"If anyone is in Christ, he is a new creature"* (2 Corinthians 5:17). That term refers to our eternal position related solely to the work of Christ on our behalf. Those who are *"in"* Christ can never be *"out of"* Christ; it does not depend on them. It applies to all who have been eternally saved.

But being "in the Lord" goes beyond that. It requires that a disciple continuously acknowledge Christ's mastery over their lives—His lordship. Maintaining that relationship therefore does depend on their on-going obedience and submission on Earth to His teaching. It is important for us to notice that these disciples were being joined in two directions - to the Lord and to each other. This was essential to their oneness, just as Israel's oneness as God's holy nation hinged on the two greatest commandments of loving the Lord and also loving each other (Matthew 22:36–40), as we looked at in chapter 10.

Continuing Steadfastly

Acts 2:42 describes the activities of that first church of God in Jerusalem. As distinct from the three one-time actions of each new convert which are described in verse 41 (gladly receiving his preaching for salvation, being baptized, and being added together), verse 42 refers to four things that they all continued to do together. This was the church in action.

- The first one mentioned is the doctrinal basis of their gathering - *"the apostles' teaching"* - what the Lord had instructed them to teach in its entirety. Adhering to that was what they had in common. If they did not get the teaching right, nothing else would be right. The Lord Jesus had instructed His apostles to teach the newly-baptized disciples *"all that I commanded you"* (Matthew 28:20). They were not to leave anything out. This included much more than telling people how they could be eternally saved through faith in Christ and how to live individual Christian lives. It certainly included those things, but it also included their need to be baptized, their need to be added to a church of God, and how to live their on-going lives of obedience and service as part of that church.

- The second thing they continued in was "*the fellowship.*" Note that in the Greek text the definite article "the" is expressly used with all four of these ongoing church activities, although this is not reflected in all English versions. It was "the apostles' teaching," "the fellowship," "the breaking of bread," and "the prayers." These were not things that they just did separately as individuals. They did them as a church, as is made explicit for example in Acts 12:5: *"Peter was kept in the prison, but prayer for him was being made fervently by the church to God.")*

- This was the defined community to which they and those in future churches of God would all belong as they adhered to that same teaching. The apostles and the others who were originally "*all with one accord in one place*" (Acts 2:2) were a community. They had been called together by the Lord to one place, for one purpose. The others who were added became part of that community. God intended that they serve Him together. They were made individually by Him, but made for fellowship with each other.

- The third activity that this community engaged in was "*the breaking of bread.*" This refers to the keeping of the Lord's Supper, the regular remembrance of the Lord Jesus in the bread and wine, as He had commanded the apostles.

- The fourth activity was "*the prayers*" —gatherings for

prayer.

Church Life in the Early Days

The verses that follow in Acts chapter 2 describe what life was like in that early Jerusalem church:

"Everyone kept feeling a sense of awe; and many wonders and signs were taking place through the apostles. And all those who had believed were together and had all things in common; and they began selling their property and possessions and were sharing them with all, as anyone might have need. Day by day continuing with one mind in the temple, and breaking bread from house to house, they were taking their meals together with gladness and sincerity of heart, praising God and having favor with all the people. And the Lord was adding to their number day by day those who were being saved." (Acts 2:43–47)

The highlights of this description include the following:

- Their awe of God, which kept them humble; they took these matters seriously.
- The evidence of God's presence in signs and wonders, which provided necessary confirmation in those days (when they had no New Testament Scriptures to rely on) that what they were doing was of the Lord (Hebrews 2:4).
- Their togetherness and sharing, meeting each other's needs—a true sense of community.

- Their steadfastness - continuing every day in their devotedness.
- Their gladness - praising God and bearing positive testimony in public.
- Their growth - the Lord was adding new disciples. Only growth that comes from God is good growth (1 Corinthians 3:7).

This was a fully functioning church of God. They were a tightly knit and devoted community. These were marvellous days. But would these things continue, or was this just a unique case? And how much of what happened then applies to us now? This is what we need to turn our attention to next.

CHAPTER THREE:
ESTABLISHING A PATTERN

"The things which you have heard from me in the presence of many witnesses, entrust these to faithful men who will be able to teach others also." (2 Timothy 2:2)

Since the experience of the first church of God in Jerusalem is intended to set a pattern for us now, even though we live almost two thousand years later, what is that pattern? Let us examine the elements that were involved in that first church in Jerusalem to determine how applicable they are.

First: Salvation

The new disciples first gladly received the word that Peter was preaching. The first spiritual event in any person's life must be coming into a personal relationship with Jesus Christ—to receive eternal salvation through faith in Him and to acknowledge Him as their Lord. God calls people to Himself through the preaching of the gospel from the Word of God (2 Thessalonians 2:14). He uses existing disciples to do that, as Peter did at Pentecost, and the whole church did subsequently: *"Those who had been scattered went about preaching the word"* (Acts 8:4). And so evangelism—spreading the good news—is a vital part of the service and activity of a church of God. Without it, there cannot be believers in Christ and disciples to form God's church.

A church with unsaved people in it cannot be a church of God. Since a church of God is the result of God calling people together, it can only consist of people who have first responded to God's call to them in the gospel. This then is the first requirement—only believers in Jesus Christ can be in a church of God. But it is not the only one.

Second: Baptism

Those newly saved disciples were then immediately baptized. The Lord had instructed that this be done, into the name of the Father and of the Son and of the Holy Spirit (Matthew 28:19). This was a baptism by immersion in water, as is evident from the later case of Philip and the eunuch from Ethiopia: *"He ordered the chariot to stop; and they both went down into the water, Philip as well as the eunuch, and he baptized him. When they came up out of the water, the Spirit of the Lord snatched Philip away"* (Acts 8:38,39).

In fact, the word baptism comes directly from the Greek word "*baptizo*," which means "to immerse." It was a common word, used for such things as dying cloth. The baptism of these disciples was a public acknowledgement of their inner spiritual experience, and of their identification with Christ in His death to sin and in His resurrection in order to *"walk in newness of life"* (Romans 6:4)[1].

When Peter began preaching to Gentiles, he first went to the city of Caesarea in response to a call to introduce this new gospel to the centurion Cornelius and his household. As he was speaking to them on that occasion, when it became apparent that those hearing had believed the gospel and received the Holy Spirit, Peter commanded them to be baptized. This shows us that being baptized is not optional but is a command, just as is the corresponding command to make and baptize new disciples.

Being baptized is the first public act of obedience that new disciples carry out to their newly found Lord. Jesus set the example Himself by being baptized by John in the Jordan River *"to fulfill all righteousness"* (Matthew 3:15). This emphasizes that a disciple's baptism is not part of how he or she becomes eternally saved, since that is by faith and confession alone (Ephesians 2:8,9; Romans 10:9),[2] but it is the response to the Lord by someone who has already been saved. Peter called it *"the answer of a good conscience toward God"* (1 Peter 3:21 NKJV).

In the Old Testament we are given an illustration of our baptism in the experience of Israel passing through the Red Sea: *"Our fathers were all under the cloud and all passed through the sea; and all were baptized into Moses in the cloud and in the sea"* (1 Corinthians 10:1,2). The people had been slaves in Egypt under the domination of Pharaoh. But God had redeemed them, by means of the blood of the Passover lambs, and separated them from the Egyptian people (Exodus 8:23). They were now about to embark on a new life together, under the leadership of Moses, and they had to be cut off from their old life in Egypt by passing through the Red Sea. This illustrates why we as disciples go through the water of baptism—to symbolize the end of our old life of living to ourselves and the domination of sin, and the start of a new life under the lordship of Jesus Christ (Romans 6:3–7). And so, baptism has two parts to it—going down into the water and coming up out of the water. The first symbolizes burial of the old self as being dead to sin; the second symbolizes being raised to live a new life to Christ in the power of the Holy Spirit.

The act of baptism itself involves three aspects—by, in, and into. It is performed "*by*" another disciple; it is "*in*" water; and it is "*into*" the name (authority) of the Father and of the Son and of the Holy Spirit (Matthew 28:19). Note that it is "name" in the singular, because of the unity of the godhead. What we are baptized "*into*" is important. Not only the words that are said at the time are important, but what is understood by them. For example, when Paul encountered some disciples in Ephesus, he discovered that they had not been baptized into that name but rather into John's baptism. He told them they needed to be baptized again, this time into [Greek: *'eis'*] the name of the Lord Jesus (Acts 19:1–5). And they were. To be baptized into the name of the Lord Jesus is to be placed completely at His disposal, as Lord of our lives, in accordance with Matthew 28:19.

Third: Addition

The third thing that happened to those new disciples at Pentecost in Jerusalem was that they were added to the disciples already gathered there, although they greatly outnumbered them—approximately three thousand to about one hundred and twenty. But additions are not in groups; each disciple had to be added individually to the group already together.

They did not "join" or become members of a church. (In fact, it is only in respect to the church the Body of Christ that we are called "members" e.g. Romans 12:4; 1 Corinthians 12:18,20,25; Ephesians 3:6). God does not want us merely to attend church or to join ourselves to a church, but to be added to His church, to become part of it. It was the existing group of disciples that added them, as directed by the Lord. Those disciples, which included the twelve apostles, *were all with one accord in one place* (Acts 2:1 NKJV). This is a significant expression; not only were they in one location but they also had a unity of purpose. They were waiting, as the Lord had told them to do before He left them: *"Gathering them together, He commanded them not to leave Jerusalem, but to wait for what the Father had promised, 'Which,' He said, 'you heard of from Me; for John baptized with water, but you will be baptized with the Holy Spirit not many days from now'"* (Acts 1:4–6).

The people *were* the church. They were *"ekklesia,"* a group of people called out by God and called together for His purpose in that place. At Pentecost they became the church of God in Jerusalem. The addition of these three thousand new disciples was a distinct step for each one of them, and it meant leaving behind whatever they had been part of previously. They could not form the church of God and still be attached to something that was contrary to it.

The Scripture goes on to say that it was actually the Lord who was adding them, and they were being added to Him: *"the Lord added to the church"* (Acts 2:47 NKJV) and *"believers were increasingly added to the Lord"* (Acts 5:14 NKJV; see also Acts 11:24). As a result of being added to the Lord, their relationship to Him is described in several places as being *"in the Lord,"* as we looked at earlier. And one benefit of this was that they became part of the *"holy temple in the Lord"* (Ephesians 2:21) which, as we saw in the last section, refers to the house of God.

Being added to a church of God involves making a commitment to the Lord Jesus and also to those in it. It is like a partnership, and that is what is meant by the words *"the fellowship"* in Acts 2:42. Casual or occasional fellowship is not an option that is offered.

Just as disciples are added to the church, sadly it is also possible for them to be put away from it [3]. For example, in his first epistle to the church at Corinth, in chapter 5, the apostle Paul wrote about the need for them to put someone out of the church because of serious sin. This shows that a church of God is something that a baptized disciple must not only be consciously added to, but may also have to be removed from. It is not just a gathering that exists to be attended or casually joined. The church does not automatically consist of all believers in a certain town. They must be added to it, and they must continue steadfastly in it. Gathering together for service is at the very heart of what a church is.

And so the church of God in Jerusalem came into existence that Pentecost day and consisted of saved, baptized, and added disciples of the Lord Jesus. And that is also the pattern for us. We have no basis to change it. At this initial stage it was co-extensive with the church the Body of Christ—all who were born again and so were members of that Body were also baptized in water and in the local church. That is the way it should be. But sadly that did not last for very long.

On-going Service

The first three steps that we have just examined—salvation, baptism, and addition—all involved actions by individuals. In each case, the disciple made a decision to do it, and each step only had to take place once. It resulted in them being part of a defined group, the church of God, and from then on their individual actions had to be guided by what they were part of.

The order of these three things is very important. Being baptized should not come before salvation; that is what led later to the practice of baptizing or sprinkling infants. Nor should being added come before salvation; the church is not for unbelievers, and churches should not have mixed congregations of believers and unbelievers. Also, addition to the church should not come before the commitment of baptism.

Acts 2:42 then describes how they began to participate in regular collective service. It included four on-going activities that were core functions of the church. Just as the sequence in which the three events in verse 41 occur is important, so is the sequence in which these four are mentioned. When we get these steps out of sequence, we get into difficulty. This sequence represents God's divine order.

Continuing in the Apostles' Teaching

It says firstly that they devoted themselves to "the apostles' teaching." A disciple by definition is one who learns, and then follows what he or she is learning. It is a never-ending process. People are not added to a church of God because of what they already know, but because of what they are willing to learn and to do.

The apostles taught everything that the Lord Jesus had taught them, just as He had instructed them to do (Matthew 28:20). It was a complete doctrine, and it formed the basis of the fellowship of which they were now a part. They did not come together for fellowship and then determine what teaching to follow. They did not form a community despite differences of doctrine. The doctrine was the basis of it all. Later, as the churches expanded to far off regions, it was a priority to maintain that uniform teaching, which was the very basis of their identity, because it had come from the Lord Jesus in the first place. Therefore, the apostles' teaching is just as relevant for us in the twenty-first century, and it continues to be the basis on which disciples should gather and serve God. We are all responsible for what we do with the apostles' teaching.

Sometimes we hear it said that doctrine does not really matter. And sometimes we hear that we should downplay doctrine because it has tended to lead to divisions among Christians. But doctrine is vital; it is the whole basis of our coming together in service for God. Doctrine is not just theory. It is what the Lord has told us to do, and so it is extremely practical. It explains to us what we should be doing to please Him. We cannot just relegate it to lesser importance.

This emphasis on the apostles' teaching inevitably meant that on-going teaching of the Word of God became an essential element in the activity of churches of God. For this purpose, teachers were raised up by the Holy Spirit (Romans 12:6,7) to follow on from the apostles. For example, the apostle Paul stressed to the young man Timothy the importance of continual sound teaching, and of correcting wrong teaching (1 Timothy 1:3; 4:11; 6:2).

Apollos was a Jewish man who was knowledgeable and eloquent in the Scriptures. When he came to Ephesus he spoke accurately what he knew, but his understanding was limited, *"being acquainted only with the baptism of John"* (Acts 18:25,26). A woman and her husband in the church there, Priscilla and Aquila, heard him speaking in the synagogue. They took him aside *"and explained to him the way of God more accurately."* As a result, Apollos came into the church of God in Ephesus, and later became an effective teacher in the church of God in Corinth (1 Corinthians 1:12; 3:6). Despite Apollos' reputation, Priscilla and Aquila were not afraid to approach him to teach him more of the way of God. It was clearly important to them. And he was obviously not above learning it and putting it into practice. That is a lovely example of the spirit of discipleship. Accurate and complete teaching of the Scriptures is vital for disciples in churches of God.

Continuing in the Fellowship

The fellowship (community) that these disciples were added to (Acts 2:42) is described in the apostle Paul's letter to the Corinthians: *"God is faithful, by whom you were called into the fellowship of His Son, Jesus Christ our Lord"* (1 Corinthians 1:9 NKJV). As we saw previously, this is a defined fellowship.

God desires unity among His people, as it reflects His own character. We live in a very individualistic age, in a society where personal differences and individual rights are considered very important. God has made us all different from one another, but He has a common purpose for us all. He is working to bring all believers into conformity with His Son (Romans 8:29). Meanwhile, He desires to unite us in our lives and service for Him. He calls us into a community that belongs to His Son. And that leaves no room for having an attitude of independence or isolation, either in our personal lives or in our church lives.

For disciples in churches of God to be His house on Earth, His "holy temple," the individual churches must be *"fitted together"* (Ephesians 2:21; *"joined together"* NKJV) in the Lord. This fellowship must be based on the teaching of the Lord Jesus through His apostles. Any union or association that is on any other basis cannot qualify. This partnership of saints and churches was shown in several practical ways in New Testament times. We saw earlier how the saints in the church in Jerusalem spent time with each other, supported each other, and met each other's practical needs. Even when the community became more widespread, this kind of fellowship continued. For example, the disciples in Antioch decided to send relief to their brethren and sisters in Judea many miles away, because of the famine there (Acts 11:29).

The inter-relationships that characterize the Body of Christ are intended to be seen within each local church of God. It is in these close quarters of community living where it can be the most challenging. We do not choose our brothers and sisters in the Lord—He does that—but the local church is the setting where our love for one another has the greatest opportunity to be worked out in practice. It has been said that church life is the laboratory where we actually learn to be Christ-like rather than just talking about it. Therefore, the pattern for us is that the churches of God must be a community, with the same teaching and with practical interaction and inter-dependency. Independent churches cannot be "churches of God."

Continuing in the Breaking of Bread

The new church then devoted itself to the regular remembrance of the Lord Jesus in the emblems of bread and wine. The Lord Jesus had originated this means for His disciples to remember Him back in the upper room (Luke 22:19), and He gave a special revelation of it later to the apostle Paul:

> *"For I received from the Lord that which I also delivered to you, that the Lord Jesus in the night in which He was betrayed took bread; and when He had given thanks, He broke it and said, 'This is My body, which is for you; do this in remembrance of Me.' In the same way He took the cup also after supper, saying, 'This cup is the new*

covenant in My blood; do this, as often as you drink it, in remembrance of Me. For as often as you eat this bread and drink the cup, you proclaim the Lord's death until He comes'" (1 Corinthians 11:23-26).

In the previous chapter, Paul had described it as a communion, a sharing: *"Is not the cup of blessing which we bless a sharing in the blood of Christ? Is not the bread which we break a sharing in the body of Christ?"* (1 Corinthians 10:16). He also referred to these emblems as *"the cup of the Lord"* (verse 21), the *"Lord's table"* (verse 21), and as *"the Lord's supper"* (11:20). It was the church that kept this remembrance. They came together as a church for this purpose (1 Corinthians 11:18). It is not prescribed as something for individual believers to engage in. Keeping this remembrance just as individual believers would be getting this third step in Acts 2:42 ahead of addition to the church (the third step in the previous verse). In fact, because these Corinthian saints were abusing this remembrance, Paul said to them, *"Do you despise the church of God?"* (1 Corinthians 11:22). They were acting in a way that damaged the harmony of those with whom they had been called together.

The breaking of bread in Acts 2:42 is different from just eating meals together, which the church in Jerusalem also did, as verse 46 shows: *"Day by day continuing with one mind in the temple, and breaking bread from house to house, they were taking their meals together with gladness and sincerity of heart"* (Acts 2:46). It was a particular spiritual activity of remembering the Lord Jesus in the way He had shown. Paul went on in chapter 11 to emphasize the importance of proper conduct and attitude at the Lord's Supper. He clearly differentiated it from just sharing food together, which is what the Corinthians were doing: *"When you meet together, it is not to eat the Lord's Supper, for in your eating each one takes his own supper first; and one is hungry and another is drunk"* (1 Corinthians 11:20,21). He told them to examine themselves before they ate to make sure they were properly discerning the significance of the emblems (because they were, in fact, only emblems); they represented the body and blood of the Lord Jesus. Because of this wrong conduct and attitude, God had been bringing judgment on them. Some of them were sick and some had even died. Obviously, the Lord takes His supper very seriously, and so should we.

In the order of activities in Acts 2:42, the breaking of bread comes before the prayers. It is focused on giving to God, and that must always come before asking for ourselves. Further worship of thanksgiving and praise follows this remembrance; it is all collective worship to God by the holy priesthood. The link between the two is seen in Hebrews chapter 10, which (as we saw earlier) describes those in the house of God drawing near to Him to worship: *"Therefore, brethren, since we have confidence to enter the holy place by the blood of Jesus, by a new and living way which He inaugurated for us through the veil, that is, His flesh, and since we have a great priest over the house of God, let us draw near with a sincere heart in full assurance of faith"* (Hebrews 10:19–22). The two bases on which we are able to come into the presence of God are *"the veil, that is His flesh"* and *"the blood of Jesus."* It is His flesh and His blood that are symbolized in the bread and wine that we partake of in the act of remembering.

The first day of the week was the day that the disciples gathered for this activity: *"We sailed from Philippi after the days of Unleavened Bread, and came to them at Troas within five days; and there we stayed seven days. On the first day of the week, when we were gathered together to break bread, Paul began talking to them, intending to leave the next day, and he prolonged his message until midnight"* (Acts 20:6,7). Paul had to stay at Troas for a whole week on his journey from Philippi to Jerusalem in order to be there for the breaking of bread. His speaking the word to the church came after that; the breaking of bread came first.

The disciples had discontinued the keeping of the Sabbath, which had been such a vital observance under the old covenant (Colossians 2:16,17). Instead they met on the first day of the week (John 19:19,26), which was the day of the Lord's resurrection (John 20:1), and it signified the new order of things that had been brought about by that pivotal event. Even in the Old Testament, the principle that God's things must come first had been clearly established. This was seen, for example, in the instructions about firstborn sons and first fruits of crops (Exodus 22:29; 23:19). The first things were devoted to God. We see this principle at work in the sin of Achan, who took the spoil of the defeat of Jericho, which was Israel's first conquest in the land of Canaan. Jericho was under a ban because its spoils belonged to God, and Achan paid for his mistake with his life (Joshua 6:17–19,24). We need to learn that we are expected to firstly give to God what belongs to Him, which is the worship of our hearts. We do it on the first day of the week, and first thing on that day.

We can see therefore that the weekly remembrance of the Lord Jesus in the symbols of bread and wine, and the related collective worship by the holy priesthood, on the first day of each week, is the pattern for each church of God today. Other service can then follow afterward.

Why is it Not for Any Believer?

When the Lord Jesus was on Earth, a large number of people believed in Him (John 2:23; 10:42). But it was to His apostles and disciples that He said, "*Do not be afraid, little flock, for your Father has chosen gladly to give you the kingdom*" (Luke 12:32). It was with the apostles that He initiated His remembrance in the bread and the wine (Luke 22:14). And it was to the apostles that He gave instruction about the kingdom of God after His resurrection (Acts 1:1–3). How were other believers to also have a part in these things? It was only by them aligning themselves with those apostles—with their teaching and their fellowship. That is what the rest of the hundred and twenty did who waited and prayed with them until the Holy Spirit came (Acts 1:13–15). That is what the three thousand did who heard and believed the gospel on the Day of Pentecost (Acts 2:41,42). That is what Saul of Tarsus did when he was converted (Acts 9:19,26,27). The little flock was becoming bigger. As it grew, and as Gentiles were added to it, as the Lord Jesus had spoken of in John 10:16, it remained one flock, with one shepherd. It was the flock of God (1 Peter 5:2,3).

These privileges are not automatically given to us as believers by virtue of salvation alone. It is available to all of us, but first we must be baptized and added to the church that is "of God", according to the apostles' teaching.

Continuing in the Prayers

The last activity listed in Acts 2:42 refers to church gatherings for prayer – *"the prayers"*. These were in addition to the saints praying individually or in groups. It was, and still is, a vital activity of a church of God. As the Lord Jesus said, quoting Isaiah 56:7, *"My house shall be called a house of prayer for all nations"* (Mark 11:17). Even before the Day of Pentecost, those who were together were devoting themselves to prayer (Acts 1:13,14). Collective prayer was a way of life for them.

We see an example of the effect of united prayer by the church in the case of Peter's rescue from prison, during a time of great persecution of the disciples in Jerusalem: *"So Peter was kept in the prison, but prayer for him was being made fervently by the church to God"* (Acts 12:5). Peter was released miraculously, by an angel coming to free him. Then he went to one of the places where the church was continuing to gather in prayer. They almost could not believe that their prayers had been answered.

Agreeing in prayer is important, as the Lord Jesus Himself explained: *"I say to you, that if two of you agree on earth about anything that they may ask, it shall be done for them by My Father who is in heaven"* (Matthew 18:19). Hebrews chapter 4 indicates that the prayers of God's collective people also involve the priestly work of Christ. He is described there as the man who totally understands our needs and feelings. Because of Him, God's throne is for us a throne of grace.

In prayer we address our requests to God as our Father, since He is the giver of all good things (James 1:17), and we offer them in the name (authority) of the Lord Jesus Christ (John 16:24). In addition to making requests, however, the scope of the prayers of God's people is extensive: *"I urge that entreaties and prayers, petitions and thanksgivings, be made on behalf of all men"* (1 Timothy 2:1).

The prayers of the saints are pictured in Revelation 5:8 as golden censers (bowls) full of incense, with a beautiful fragrance that constantly rises up to God. While disciples may gather to pray for particular things at particular times on Earth, it is as though their prayers are all collected in bowls, and the sweet smell constantly rises to God for His enjoyment. He is not bound by restrictions of time or location, as we are. And so we see that the regular gathering of disciples in a church of God for prayer is a vital part of their on-going activity. It is part of the pattern for us today.

The Order of Acts 2:42

Just as we saw earlier in the chapter that the sequence of things in verse 41 is vital, so is the sequence of verse 42. Problems develop when we change God's order of things. For example, if we put the fellowship before the teaching—that is, if we do not gather based on the teaching—then the gathering itself becomes more important than the teaching. This can lead a church to adapting or adjusting doctrine to preserve itself as an organization. That is what the Reformers of the fourteenth to sixteenth Centuries claimed the church was doing at that time.

Then, for example, if we put the breaking of bread before the fellowship, we include in the Lord's Supper those who are not in churches of God. If we put the prayers (or other service for God, such as preaching the gospel) before the breaking of bread, God is not being given His part first. In the pattern that has been left for us, this divine order is vital. But was it continued as the churches began to multiply and as disciples began to spread out geographically? Let's look at that question next.

CHAPTER FOUR:
REPRODUCING THE PATTERN

"And so I direct in all the churches." (1 Corinthians 7:17)

Initially there was just one church of God, in Jerusalem, although it often gathered in multiple locations—various homes, and also public places such as the Solomon's porch area of the temple grounds. But eventually many churches of God were established throughout the Roman Empire as the community expanded. It also became more culturally diverse, as Gentiles were added. But it remained as one community. Its united adherence to the full teaching of the faith remained paramount.

Throughout the book of the Acts of the Apostles, as well as the epistles, it is noteworthy how diligent the disciples were in maintaining this unity. It would have been very easy for them to have become fragmented and separate, especially with long distances between them, limited methods of communication, and the cultural differences between Gentiles and Jews. But they worked hard at it by various means, such as visitation, written epistles, an elders' and apostles' conference, mutual prayer, and the sending of practical support to those in need.

The Persecution

The persecution of the disciples by the Jews (such as Saul of Tarsus) became so severe that almost the whole church at Jerusalem fled in various directions (Acts 8:1). Disciples became known initially as "the Way" (Acts 9:2; 24:14) and were regarded as a sect. Later they become known as "Christians" (Acts 11:26)—that is, followers of the Messiah. However the apostles did not leave Jerusalem, and so all these other saints were now on their own as they established churches in other places. The church in Jerusalem became a lot smaller in a hurry.

First of all, a new development started in Samaria, a region a few miles north of Jerusalem, where Philip the evangelist had gone (Acts 8:5–12). People were being saved and baptized, and so the apostles Peter and John went to Samaria to link the group there with the existing ones in Jerusalem and elsewhere in the region of Judea. Maintaining this unity of teaching and communications was vital, and it was up to the apostles to lay the foundation of the uniform teaching. The churches in Samaria were not a new movement; they were becoming a new part of the existing fellowship.

Meanwhile, back in Jerusalem, an eager young orthodox Jew from Tarsus by the name of Saul, who was already a member of the elite Pharisees, began a personal campaign to stamp out these disciples in churches of God. He imprisoned them and sentenced them to death. He thought that what they were doing was sacrilegious. It says that he made havoc of the church (Acts 8:3). He himself said later that he *"persecuted the church of God"* (1 Corinthians 15:9). But Christ said about it at the time: *"Why are you persecuting Me?"* (Acts 9:4). It is clear that Christ takes the church of God very personally.

After Jerusalem, he intended to track these disciples down as far as Damascus, about a hundred miles to the northeast, but he was miraculously converted on the way (Acts 9). Saul's conversion was a major turning point, and an example of God using adversity to further His own purposes, as He so often does. From being a persecutor of the churches, he (referred to as Paul the apostle) would become the major founder and builder of churches of God throughout the Gentile part of the Roman Empire. He would have to suffer a great deal personally in doing so. He referred to himself as *"a wise master builder"* (1 Corinthians 3:10).

Staying United While Spreading Out

Largely through the efforts of a man nicknamed Barnabas, a great many people were *"added to the Lord"* in the city of Antioch, well over two hundred miles north of Galilee (Acts 11:24). It had started with the persecuted disciples arriving there from Jerusalem and spreading the Word. Barnabas went up from Jerusalem to establish a church there. Then he recognized that he needed help in teaching and supporting these new disciples, and so he continued on to Tarsus, which was not far away, and brought back Paul, who had been back there in his home town for several years. It was while Paul and Barnabas were both in Antioch that they were called by the Holy Spirit to engage in enlarging the work (Acts 13:2).

During this time of expansion, we see several instances of how these increasingly spread-out churches stayed united. For example, a prophet visited Antioch from Jerusalem (Acts 21:10). Prophets with direct revelation from God were used in those days to complement the apostles (Ephesians 4:11), as there were as yet no written New Testament Scriptures. Another practical example of their unity was when the saints in Antioch sent relief to their fellow-saints in Jerusalem and Judaea when a famine was imminent (Acts 11:29,30). There was obviously communication between these churches.

Meanwhile in Jerusalem, king Herod Agrippa spearheaded a new wave of the persecution. It cost the apostle James his life. It looked as if Peter would suffer a similar fate, but the church constantly prayed for him (Acts 12:5). From this point on James, the brother of the Lord Jesus, became more prominent in the life of the church in Jerusalem. In fact, it was during this phase that we begin to see the transition from apostles to other elders (Acts 11:30), and the need for there to be elders in each church to care for the saints (Titus 1:5).

Maintaining the Churches

The apostle Paul often revisited many of the newly established churches. He knew that they needed follow-up teaching and support. It was not enough to establish them and then leave them on their own. This on-going building up was a vital part of maintaining these churches in the faith as they multiplied and spread out. It was important that they stayed part of the one fellowship, and did not become just independent churches, practicing what each thought best.

Acts chapter 15 describes a landmark event—a gathering of apostles and elders from Jerusalem and Antioch to resolve a question as to the teaching of the Lord about what was required for disciples: whether circumcision was necessary, as it had been under Judaism. Had they not resolved it by consultation, the issue could have caused a severe breach in the young community.

It could have led to them no longer being the one fellowship of God's Son. Quite apart from the issue itself, the process they used is particularly enlightening. The apostles were involved because it had been given to them to lay down the foundation teaching; the other elders were involved because they would have the on-going responsibility to care for the churches and safeguard the teaching in the absence of the apostles. From this gathering we get the pattern of elders' meetings as the process for discovering or confirming the teaching of the Lord, so as to maintain unity of teaching and practice throughout the churches of God.

After this conference Paul and his companion Silas travelled back through the churches, informing them of the decision: *"Now while they were passing through the cities, they were delivering the decrees which had been decided upon by the apostles and elders who were in Jerusalem, for them to observe. So the churches were being strengthened in the faith, and were increasing in number daily"* (Acts 16:4,5). They arrived in Jerusalem divided but they returned home united, by which the saints were encouraged and strengthened.

As the New Testament epistles began to be disseminated, the faith was being delivered in writing gradually to the saints. By the time Jude wrote about it in his epistle, the faith had been *"once for all delivered to the saints"* (Jude verse 3). It had not been delivered all at once, but by then it had been delivered completely. The foundation had been laid and will remain until the end of the age when the Lord returns (Matthew 28:20). These epistles now constitute for us a great written heritage.

The apostles' teaching has never been revoked; it applies every bit as much today. Romans 6:17 expresses it this way: *"But thanks be to God that though you were slaves of sin, you became obedient from the heart to that form of teaching to which you were committed."* This shows that, not only was the teaching delivered to the saints (Jude verse 3), but the saints were delivered to it—to the "form" (the word means a mould or pattern) of teaching to which they were to conform themselves. As each church of God had been planted, it had come out of the same mould of teaching, and this resulted in a network of consistent inter-dependent churches. It was among such churches that the Lord Jesus walked, as Revelation 1 describes. He was able to walk among them as long as they would submit to His authority. The disciples had to be fitted into this divine pattern and teaching; the teaching could not be adapted to their own views or preferences.

The Pattern Set for Us

As we look back over the early history of the churches of God as recorded in the New Testament, we see a number of important trends over the course of those critically important forty or so years:

- It began with about one hundred and twenty people being all assembled with one accord in one place in Jerusalem, but it progressed to being a network of inter-dependent churches throughout dozens of towns and cities in the Roman Empire. They were a community, a fellowship.

- It began being restricted to Jews, the small remnant of Israel who believed in and were committed to follow their Messiah, but it progressed to being a universal, multi-cultural community to which persons of all racial backgrounds and social status were admitted.

- It began with the Word of God being revealed orally by apostles such as Peter and Paul, as well as by prophets such as Judas and Silas (Acts 15:32), and authenticated by miraculous signs. It progressed to a written record of events and teaching, which constituted the New Testament and which, together with the Old Testament, formed the authoritative "canon" (standard) of Scripture.

- It began with the Lord Jesus instructing His apostles after His resurrection to teach *all that I commanded you*, which became known as *the apostles' doctrine* (teaching), and then as *the faith once for all delivered to the saints,* which was the basis of the unity of the community.

- It began with twelve apostles of the Lord Jesus, who had seen Him and received His commandments personally, and progressed to a unique system of governance by a collective elderhood.

It is this last matter of leadership in the churches to which we now need to turn our attention.

CHAPTER FIVE: LEADERSHIP IN THE CHURCHES

"To all the saints in Christ Jesus who are in Philippi, including the overseers and deacons." (Philippians 1:1)

The church the Body of Christ has no human leaders. It is a spiritual entity where each member of the Body is directly under the headship of Christ. He is the Head of the Body, and each member has equal status in it: *"There is neither Jew nor Greek, there is neither slave nor free man, there is neither male nor female; for you are all one in Christ Jesus"* (Galatians 3:28). However, from the outset, human leadership was needed (and was provided) in churches of God, with distinct roles.

Apostles

The Lord had given direct responsibility to His eleven apostles before His departure. Then Matthias was added, and later Paul. They were *"apostles of our Lord Jesus Christ"* (Jude verse 17). Peter and Paul both wrote more than once in their epistles that they were "apostles of Jesus Christ," highlighting that it was by His divine appointment. Paul also said, *"Am I not an apostle? ... Have I not seen Jesus Christ our Lord?"* (1 Corinthians 9:1). They carried authority as those who had seen Him and received His commandments personally.

The apostles had particular responsibility in the early days to make the major decisions (such as arranging for the appointment of men in the Jerusalem church to oversee the care of the widows,

Acts 6:1–4), and to mentor other elders (e.g. Titus 1:4). The *"apostles teaching"* (Acts 2:42) was to be relayed to others as Paul described in 2 Timothy 2:2, *"The things which you have heard from me in the presence of many witnesses, entrust these to faithful men who will be able to teach others also."* However, once they passed on, no others were appointed to succeed them as apostles.

"Apostolic succession" is not something that is taught in Scripture. The only case of this was Matthias replacing Judas, as described in Acts 1:26, to restore the number of apostles to twelve. In addition, the apostle Paul was specially raised up, as *"one untimely born"* (1 Corinthians 15:8), to take the message to the Gentiles as well as to the Jews (Acts 9:15). [4] And so by the time most of them had died, the work of apostles was done. The foundation teaching had been passed on to the churches in its entirety (Jude verse 3).

The apostles played the pivotal role in the beginning. They were the nucleus around which the kingdom of God was developed after the Lord's departure. They were the ones who were told to go and make disciples, which is how the kingdom was to be populated. Therefore, as disciples were made and baptized, they had to join themselves with those apostles, adhering to their teaching, to be in the kingdom of God. There was to be one flock of God, under one shepherd, even after Gentiles were added (John 10:14).

Elders (Overseers or Bishops)

It was over that flock that overseers were appointed by the Holy Spirit in the churches of God, to care for them as under-shepherds (Acts 20:28,29; 1 Peter 5:2,3). It is Acts 11:30 that we read explicitly about elders in a church of God for the first time. Just as there had been elders in Israel in the Old Testament, men who played an important part in the governance of the people, so elders were appointed to govern and care for churches of God. In fact, the absence of elders in any church was a lack that needed to be remedied, as Paul instructed Titus: *"For this reason I left you in Crete, that you should set in order the things that are lacking, and appoint elders in every city as I commanded you"* (Titus 1:5 NKJV). More than one elder was to be appointed in each place.

Because existing elders were the ones who appointed other elders, specifications were given as to the type of men they should appoint. (These requirements are listed in 1 Timothy 3:2–7 and Titus 1:6–8.) However, as Paul pointed out to the elders of the church in Ephesus when he met with them at Miletus, it is the Holy Spirit who actually appoints them (Acts 20:28,29). It is then men's responsibility to recognize where He has done that and to implement that appointment.

Elders are to work collectively, and the unity of the elderhood is essential both within one assembly and across the entire fellowship of assemblies. Together they must safeguard the teaching of the Lord, *"holding fast the faithful word which is in accordance with the teaching, so that he will be able both to exhort in sound doctrine and to refute those who contradict"* (Titus 1:9).

Otherwise the house of God could not continue to have uniform teaching and be *"the pillar and support of the truth"* (1 Timothy 3:15).

This unity of the elderhood is the unity of the whole elderhood, not just a subset of it (such as exists in a hierarchy, where some decisions are made "at the top"). Rule is by elders in each church, who consult together to maintain unity of teaching and practice. Decisions of such elders together are binding; otherwise the unity would not be maintained. The application of the decisions is in the local churches, by the local elders, and requires their submission to those collective decisions. United elderhood is a unique and divinely-designed form of rule.

> There are several Scriptures addressed to elders, or written about them, that show what their particular responsibilities are:

> • The overall leadership and governance of the church.

> *"Obey your leaders and submit to them, for they keep watch over your souls as those who will give an account. Let them do this with joy and not with grief, for this would be unprofitable for you"* (Hebrews 13:17).

> • The spiritual care of the saints.

"Take care of the church of God" (1 Timothy 3:5). *"Admonish the unruly, encourage the fainthearted, help the weak, be patient with everyone"* (1 Thessalonians 5:14). *"Shepherd the flock of God among you, exercizing oversight ..."* (1 Peter 5:2).

- Teaching the Scriptures.

"Prescribe and teach these things" (1 Timothy 4:11). *"The things which you have heard from me in the presence of many witnesses, entrust these to faithful men who will be able to teach others also"* (2 Timothy 2:2,3).

- Guarding the doctrine.

"Reprove, rebuke, exhort, with great patience and instruction" (2 Timothy 4:2). *"Guard what has been entrusted to you"* (1 Timothy 6:20). *"They were delivering the decrees which had been decided upon by the apostles and elders who were in Jerusalem, for them to observe"* (Acts 16:4).

- Recognizing gift, for giving responsibility in the church.

"Do not neglect the spiritual gift within you, which was bestowed on you through prophetic utterance with the laying on of hands by the presbytery" (1 Timothy 4:14) [5]. *"Set in order the things that are lacking, and appoint elders"* (Titus1:5 NKJV).

- Ensuring the care of the needy.

"To send a contribution for the relief of the brethren living in Judea. This they also did, sending it ... to the elders" (Acts 11:29,30). *"You must help the weak"* (Acts 20:35).

- Resolving conflict in the church.

"See that no one repays another with evil for evil, but always seek after that which is good for one another and for all people" (1 Thessalonians 5:15).

- Guiding the church in applying discipline, excommunication, and restoration.

"Those who continue in sin, rebuke in the presence of all, so that the rest also will be fearful of sinning" (1 Timothy 5:20). *"Reject a factious man after a first and second warning"* (Titus 3:10).

- Being role models.

"Proving to be examples to the flock" (1 Peter 5:3). *"Be on guard for yourselves and for all the flock, among which the Holy Spirit has made you overseers, to shepherd the church of God which He purchased with His own blood"* (Acts 20:28).

Because oversight work is a united work, it requires continual consultation and co-operation, including subjection to one another. 3 John verses 9,10 refer to the case of Diotrephes who was putting people out of the church because they wanted to receive brethren among them, which he was prohibiting. This shows the potential danger of an individual man having the authority. Overseers working together show the uniting effect of the Holy Spirit in what they do.

Matters affecting individual saints concern the overseers in that local church, since they are charged with the care of that church (1 Timothy 3:5). Matters of doctrine and uniform practice need to go to levels of the oversight beyond the local church for agreement (such as occurred in Acts 15). The conference of apostles and elders in Acts 15 sets the pattern for this process. The conclusion on that occasion was expressed as follows: "*It seemed good to the Holy Spirit, and to us*" (Acts 15:28). Afterwards the apostle Paul and Silas (an elder) went around the churches communicating the decision, described as "decrees." The result was the up-building of the churches (Acts 16:5).

The early churches were grouped in districts or regions. We read of the churches in Galatia (1 Corinthians 16:1), Macedonia (2 Corinthians 8:1), Judea (Galatians 1:22), and Asia (Revelation 1:4). Overseers of these districts may well have met as they found it necessary in order to deal with matters of mutual concern.

[6] If the fellowship of churches had not been based on united adherence to the apostles' teaching (*"the unity of the faith"*, Ephesians 4:13), their inter-dependence and mutual accountability would not have been necessary. They could each have operated on their own. The local overseers would not have needed to pursue unity beyond their own church. But this was not the divine pattern.

The relationship of overseers to the rest of the saints in a church of God is described as being "*among*" them, and a warning is given to them not to abuse their authority: "*Shepherd the flock of God among you, exercising oversight not under compulsion, but voluntarily, according to the will of God; and not for sordid gain, but with eagerness; nor yet as lording it over those allotted to your charge, but proving to be examples to the flock. And when the Chief Shepherd appears, you will receive the unfading crown of glory*" (1 Peter 5:2–4).

On the other hand, the saints are accountable to their overseers. They are to respect their overseers' authority and to imitate their faith as seen in their godly lives:

> "*Remember those who led you, who spoke the word of God to you; and considering the result of their conduct, imitate their faith ... Obey your leaders and submit to them, for they keep watch over your souls as those who will give an account. Let them do this with joy and not with grief, for this would be unprofitable for you.*" (Hebrews 13:7,17).

The church of God in Thessalonica was told that their overseers were "*over you in the Lord*" (1 Thessalonians 5:12). Here again is the expression "in the Lord" which, as we discovered earlier, refers to those who are gathered in obedience to the Lord in God's churches in the kingdom of God. Obviously, these overseers were not over other believers who were not in the church. There are no overseers or elders over the church the Body of Christ. As we saw previously, the expression "in the Lord" does not automatically apply to all believers in the Body.

Deacons

In addition to overseers, deacons were appointed in the early churches: *"To all the saints in Christ Jesus who are in Philippi, including the overseers and deacons"* (Philippians 1:1). Their qualifications are shown in 1 Timothy 3:8–13. The word deacon means a servant, and these men were appointed to serve the saints. As we saw earlier, this is a different word (Greek: *"diakonos"*) than the word used for service to God, such as worship (Greek: *"leitourgos"*). Christ is referred to as a minister (servant) in both capacities—towards men and women when He was on Earth, and towards God on our behalf in heaven now:

> *"The Son of Man did not come to be served, but to serve* ['diakonos'], *and to give His life a ransom for many"* (Matthew 20:28).

> *"We have such a high priest ... a minister* ['leitourgos'] *in the sanctuary...He has obtained a more excellent ministry"* (Hebrews 8:1,2,6).

All men and women in a church of God have an opportunity to be servants of the church. For example, the woman Phoebe and the man Tychicus are both described in this way (Romans 16:1; Ephesians 6:21). However, it appears that only men were recognized in this position, where it was their on-going responsibility. In 1 Timothy 3:8, it is explicit that those who are recognized as deacons should be men and, since this is a leadership position, it is consistent with the limitations given in 1 Timothy 2:12 regarding the role of women in the church. [7]

Pastors

Many Christian churches today have one or more ordained pastors, often professionally trained and qualified. They often undertake much of the service of the church, with the congregation sometimes being a relatively passive audience. However, all saints in the churches of God are part of the priesthood and should be active in its service. There is no distinction given in Scripture between a clergy and a congregation.

In the New Testament churches of God, the responsibility of pastoring (caring for) the saints belonged to the overseers. As pastors ("shepherds") they were accountable to the Lord Jesus as the Chief Shepherd: *"I exhort the elders among you ... shepherd the flock of God among you ... when the Chief Shepherd appears, you will receive the unfading crown of glory"* (1 Peter 5:1–4).

CHAPTER SIX: BUILDING UP THE CHURCHES

"I laid a foundation, and another is building on it. But each man must be careful how he builds on it." (1 Corinthians 3:10)

God is a builder of churches, and He uses men and women to do the building. We therefore can have the privilege of building something of permanent value for God. And if we do, we will be rewarded for it: *"Each man's work will become evident; for the day will show it because it is to be revealed with fire, and the fire itself will test the quality of each man's work. If any man's work which he has built on it remains, he will receive a reward"* (1 Corinthians 3:13,14). The honour however goes to the builder, who is God (Hebrews 3:3,4).

God builds His house in three directions at once—"on," "together," and "up." Let's look at each of these.

Building On

"Having been built on the foundation of the apostles and prophets, Christ Jesus Himself being the corner stone" (Ephesians 2:20).

Firstly, for it to be a church of God, a church must be built *on* the right foundation, which is the teaching of the Lord Jesus Christ, as we have seen. The apostle Paul said to the church at Corinth, *"I laid a foundation, and another is building on it. But each man must be careful how he builds on it. For no man can lay a foundation other than the one which is laid, which is Jesus Christ.*

Now if anyone builds on the foundation with gold, silver, precious stones, wood, hay, straw, each man's work will become evident ..." (1 Corinthians 3:10–13).

Like the first one in Jerusalem, therefore, a church of God must be built based on what the apostles originally taught, which is the entire body of teaching that they received from the Lord. Any church that is not based on this full teaching of Christ as given to His apostles cannot be a church of God, and therefore cannot be part of the house of God, which is the pillar and support of the truth (1 Timothy 3:15). God only gives His name to what He originates. This teaching corresponds to the first element that the church in Jerusalem devoted themselves to, as listed in Acts 2:42. (Appendix B identifies some key elements of this foundational teaching, which came to be referred to as "the faith.")

Building Together

"In whom the whole building, being fitted together, is growing into a holy temple in the Lord" (Ephesians 2:21).

Secondly, a church of God must be built together with other churches of God to form a united community. This is *"the unity of the faith"* that Paul wrote about (Ephesians 4:13). It is not enough that a church of Christians be doing the right things; it must also be connected to the others. It must be part of the one community. This corresponds to the second item in Acts 2:42—"the fellowship." God's purposes are collective, and He desires unity among His people.

It must have been difficult for those early churches to stay united in doctrine and fellowship in the first century. They did not have the means of travel and communications that we have, and they were constantly facing opposition. As mentioned previously, they used several means, that apply similarly to us today:

- Consistent oral teaching in all the churches (Acts 20:2). The apostle Paul told the Corinthians that he ordained the same things in every church (1 Corinthians 7:17).
- Letters (epistles) sent, read, and circulated among the churches, constituting a body of authoritative Christian literature (Colossians 4:16).
- Visits to the churches, and saints being commended from one to another for full fellowship (Acts 18:27; Romans 16:1).
- Prayer for saints in all the churches. The apostle Paul often wrote that he was praying for the saints in the churches; they were his greatest concern (Colossians 1:3; 2 Corinthians 11:28).
- Relief to meet financial need in other churches (Acts 11:29,30). Good works were important (Galatians 2:10), and their first priority was to be those of "the household of the faith" (Galatians 6:10).
- Support for the spread of the gospel in other places. Paul praised the Philippians for their participation in the gospel (Philippians 1:5). In addition to preaching it locally themselves, they were praying for his work and were supporting it financially.
- Unity of oversight, by consulting with each other about matters which could otherwise divide them, to learn the

mind of the Spirit (Acts 15:28).

There are many references in the epistles to this maintenance of unity, especially in the writings of the apostle Paul, who travelled widely among the churches:

- *"just as I teach everywhere in every church"* (1 Corinthians 4:17);
- *"so I direct in all the churches"* (1 Corinthians 7:17);
- *"we have no other practice, nor have the churches of God"* (1 Corinthians 11:16);
- *"as in all the churches of the saints"* (1 Corinthians 14:33);
- *"through all the churches"* (2 Corinthians 8:18);
- *"the daily pressure on me of concern for all the churches"* (2 Corinthians 11:28);
- *"have it also read in the church of the Laodiceans"* (Colossians 4:16);
- *"you ... became imitators of the churches of God in Christ Jesus that are in Judea"* (1 Thessalonians 2:14); and
- *"what the Spirit says to the churches"* (Revelation 2:7,11,17, 29; 3:6,13,22).

Building Up

"You also, as living stones, are being built up as a spiritual house" (1 Peter 2:5).

Thirdly, a church of God must be being built up through spiritual life and service. A church that does not gather regularly for the breaking of bread or for the prayers, for example (the third and fourth items in Acts 2:42), cannot be a church of God. A church that specializes in only some selected aspect of the service of God but does not engage in the others cannot be a church of God.

In addition, a church of God can become spiritually dead (although that description may not apply to every saint in it). The Lord Jesus warned the church in Sardis: *"I know your deeds, that you have a name that you are alive, but you are dead. Wake up, and strengthen the things that remain, which were about to die; for I have not found your deeds completed in the sight of My God. So remember what you have received and heard; and keep it, and repent"* (Revelation 3:1-3).

Similarly, He warned the church in Ephesus: *"I have this against you, that you have left your first love. Therefore remember from where you have fallen, and repent and do the deeds you did at first; or else I am coming to you and will remove your lampstand out of its place—unless you repent. Yet this you do have, that you hate the deeds of the Nicolaitans, which I also hate"* (Revelation 2:4–6). He was saying that, unless they responded and changed, they would no longer be recognized by God, even if they continued to meet and carry out certain activity.

In effect these three aspects of God's building work define what is a church of God. They are the criteria whereby we can assess whether a gathering of baptized disciples is in fact a "church of God":

- Is it built ON the full teaching of the Lord Jesus Christ, as passed on by the apostles, and recorded in the New

Testament? and

- Is it built TOGETHER to be united in teaching and operation with other churches of God as the fellowship of God's Son? and

- Is it built UP through authentic spiritual activity and service?

Spiritual Gifts

The work of edifying (spiritually building up) a church is carried out by the saints in it exercising their God-given spiritual gifts: *"There are varieties of gifts, but the same Spirit. And there are varieties of ministries, and the same Lord. There are varieties of effects, but the same God who works all things in all persons. But to each one is given the manifestation of the Spirit for the common good"* (1 Corinthians 12:4–7).

From this passage of Scripture we can see three things that are linked together, involving all three persons of the godhead:

- our ministries (service) for the Lord;
- our gifts from the Holy Spirit to enable us to carry out those ministries; and
- the activities and arrangements in which they are carried out, as co-ordinated by God.

The gifts are given by the Spirit to all members of the Body, and given for the benefit of us all. Romans 12:6–8 and 1 Corinthians 12:4–11 are two Scriptures in particular that list a number of such gifts. A fully-functioning church of God gives ample scope for the exercise of various gifts by the saints in it. The church in

Corinth was described by the apostle as coming short in no gift (1 Corinthians 1:7). The particular emphasis in service that any one church is able to give is largely determined by the gifts that those in it have been provided with. The gifts are intended to be used in harmony with each other for the strengthening of the church and its work.

However service that is directed towards God, rather than to each other, is not a matter of specialized gift. Worship and prayer are for all to engage in. They are not restricted to certain saints.

The Distinct Roles of Men and Women

In the Body of Christ there is no gender distinction—"*no male or female*" (Galatians 3:28). However, in a church of God there are male and female distinctions. The apostle Paul wrote to the church at Corinth about being God's sons and daughters (2 Corinthians 6:16-18). And he said to them, "*I want you to understand that Christ is the head of every man, and the man is the head of a woman, and God is the head of Christ*" (1 Corinthians 11:3). There is a clear order here—from God to Christ, to man, to woman. In each pairing, the relationship is characterized by one being the head and the other showing subjection, all to the glory of God.

Christ Himself was the perfect example of this. His entire ministry on Earth was for the purpose of glorifying His Father. Similarly, it is the man's role to glorify Christ (and in so doing to glorify God), and the woman's to glorify the man (1 Corinthians 11:7). However, there is also inter-dependency (1 Corinthians 11:11). A woman is given hair as her glory, but in her role in the church she is to cover it. In showing subjection to the man in a church setting, a woman is in effect showing it to Christ and to God when the assembly is together in divine order. Similarly, by showing His subjection to Christ, a man also shows it to God. [8]

This distinction in roles in the service of the church is to be demonstrated in several distinct ways, the apostle stated. These are summarized as follows:

Men	Women
HEAD COVERING	
(1 Corinthians 11:4–16)	
Their heads are to remain uncovered while they are speaking, either to God or a message from God; they thereby show their distinction from the women.	Their heads are to be covered in these situations. Their head covering is worn as a sign that they are under authority.
SPEAKING WHEN THE CHURCH IS GATHERED AS A CHURCH	
(1 Corinthians 11:18; 14:34; 1 Timothy 2:8)	
Men are the ones to participate audibly in the church gatherings by speaking on behalf of the assembly in worship and prayer, and in speaking to the assembly.	The women remain silent (do not speak out individually) in these gatherings, although they join in the collective singing and saying the "Amen."
POSITIONS OF AUTHORITY	
(1 Corinthians 14:26,34; 1 Timothy 2:8)	
Men are the ones to teach and lead. Elders and deacons are to be men.	The women are not to teach or have authority over the men.

Some of these requirements are quite different from what many societies today consider appropriate. However, they represent God's prescription for conduct in His kingdom, and they have great significance. They should not be dismissed as having only cultural relevance in the first century.

Behaviour and Discipline

Whether we focus on our relationship to God in the churches of God, in the house of God, or in the kingdom of God, a consistent theme emerges from Scripture—holiness and godly behaviour is expected: *"Holiness befits Your house, O Lord, forevermore"* (Psalm 93:5). There are consequences if we live otherwise. We are told to put to death the fleshly nature in us that leads to sin (Galatians 5:24). We are also told that, when we sin, we are to confess that sin to God (1 John 1:9); we are then given the promise that God will unconditionally forgive us and cleanse us from all unrighteousness.

When a problem exists between two people in the church, the process is given to us for dealing with it. In giving this instruction, the Lord dealt with two related situations:

- Where one person has a difficulty with someone else in the church:

"If your brother sins, go and show him his fault in private; if he listens to you, you have won your brother. But if he does not listen to you, take one or two more with you, so that by the mouth of two or three witnesses every fact may be confirmed. If he refuses to listen to

*them, tell it to the church; and if he refuses to listen even
to the church, let him be to you as a Gentile and a tax
collector"* (Matthew 18:15–17); and

- Where someone knows that another person has
  difficulty with them:

*"If you are presenting your offering at the altar, and
there remember that your brother has something
against you, leave your offering there before the altar
and go; first be reconciled to your brother, and then come
and present your offering"* (Matthew 5:23,24).

In both cases, it is imperative that the matter be dealt with,
and dealt with promptly. In the Matthew 18 case, it explicitly
says that the situation could become serious enough to warrant
excommunication from the church – *"let him be to you as a
Gentile and a tax collector."*

Sin by a brother or sister in a church taints that church, and
the church has a responsibility to address it. The apostle Paul
compared sin in an assembly to leaven (yeast) that spreads to
others. Sin can contaminate those around it. The church in
Corinth was told to purge out the sin in it (1 Corinthians 5:6,7).
This chapter addresses a particular case of immorality in a
church, and the apostle Paul was very explicit about how the
saints were to deal with it. He said: *"Put away from yourselves the
evil person"* (1 Corinthians 5:13). He was instructing the church
to excommunicate the man, to put him out of the church, *"for*

the destruction of the flesh" (verse 5). It would appear from 2 Corinthians chapter 2, verse 7 that the man later repented and was restored to the church.

1 Corinthians 5:11 lists sins for which excommunication applies. There are similar lists of serious sins in 1 Corinthians 6:9,10; Galatians 5:19–21, and Ephesians 5:5, where the consequence of a person being excommunicated is described as them losing their inheritance in the kingdom of God. If sin is not dealt with in a church of God it may incur the judgment of God. For example, the Lord said to the church in Thyatira:

> *"You tolerate the woman Jezebel, who calls herself a prophetess, and she teaches and leads My bond-servants astray so that they commit acts of immorality and eat things sacrificed to idols. I gave her time to repent, and she does not want to repent of her immorality. Behold, I will throw her on a bed of sickness, and those who commit adultery with her into great tribulation, unless they repent of her deeds. And I will kill her children with pestilence, and all the churches will know that I am He who searches the minds and hearts; and I will give to each one of you according to your deeds"* (Revelation 2:20–23).

He was protecting the holiness of His house.

Edification

The apostle Paul was continually engaged in the building up (edifying) of what God was building in each place. He wrote to the church at Colosse: *"As you have received Christ Jesus the Lord, so walk in Him, having been firmly rooted and now being built up in Him and established in your faith, just as you were instructed, and overflowing with gratitude"* (Colossians 2:6,7). The churches were a pre-occupation with him, as he admitted: *"There is the daily pressure on me of concern for all the churches"* (2 Corinthians 11:28).

Churches of God are intended to provide support for the disciples in them, providing care, fellowship, encouragement, and opportunity for service. This is what God looks for in His churches, and it is how the saints in them show their love to Him. We are not expected to live our Christian lives alone.

Many church organizations in the world today are highly specialized. They focus on one or two important aspects of the work of God, such as missions, charitable activity, or preaching the Word. However, a scriptural church of God is intended to be a full-scope church, exhibiting all aspects of the life and service of disciples. Thus we should expect to see it regularly engaged in

- Worship;
- Prayer;
- Making (and baptizing and adding) disciples;
- Teaching the Word of God;
- Supporting and caring for each other;
- Doing good to others outside the church; and

- Enjoying fellowship with each other.

All of this, of course, must be more than just activity. It must be soundly based on genuine devotion to the Lord Jesus.

CHAPTER SEVEN: MAKING THE CONNECTIONS

"You are Christ's body"; "you are a temple of God"; "He has made us to be a kingdom." (1 Corinthians 12:27; 1 Corinthians 3:16; Revelation 1:6)

As we discover the truth of churches of God from Scripture—that is, how disciples ought to gather to serve the Lord in these days—we will realize that it is not an isolated truth. While it is confined to the present period from Pentecost to the Lord's return, it is all part of an integrated pattern that reflects the very character of God. This truth about God's church is distinct from, and yet connected to, the spiritual realities of (a) the church the Body of Christ, (b) the house of God, and (c) the kingdom of God.

Connected to the Body of Christ

The question might be asked: Since a church of God does not simply consist of local members of the Body of Christ who gather together, what is the connection between the churches of God and the church the Body of Christ? Both of them have the name "church," meaning people called out to be together by God. Why then does He call out two churches?

Paul wrote to the church of God in Corinth, *"You are Christ's body"* (1 Corinthians 12:27) (not "you are *'the'* body of Christ," because they were only part of it). Each disciple in the church at Corinth was also a member of that Body, and so he told them they were not to act independently of one another. He wrote this in the context of them using their various spiritual gifts, which they had each received from the Holy Spirit. Each gift was to be used in the church at Corinth in conjunction with each other's, without regarding one as more important than the other. What was important was the overall effect. The over-riding purpose of these gifts was not just that each person would feel fulfilled, but that all the saints would be built up (Ephesians 4:12, 16). The apostle said to the church in Corinth, *"Since you are zealous of spiritual gifts, seek to abound for the edification of the church"* (1 Corinthians 14:12).

The Body of Christ is a spiritual union that pertains to the perfect relationship that exists among believers, and between them and their Head, who is Christ. It focuses on the inter-relationships and inter-dependencies of those believers. God intends that all members of Christ's Body on Earth be in churches of God to obediently live and serve there together, in full accordance with the Lord's commands and in full harmony with each other. In fact the only legitimate way that full unity of living members of the Body can be exhibited in practice is in scriptural churches of God. And so God calls disciples into His churches as the place where they can primarily function in relation to others.

For someone to say that membership in the Body of Christ is all that is required to be in a scriptural church of God is to ignore the clear teaching of Scripture about the need for baptism, addition, and continuing steadfastly as the church in Jerusalem did. The "Great Commission" from the Lord Jesus included teaching disciples to do *"all"* that He commanded (Matthew 28:18–20). This is not just a nice ideal but a prerequisite for serving God acceptably.

When Paul addressed the saints in the churches of God in both Ephesus and Colosse, he described them as those who were "faithful in Christ." They were not only believers in Christ; they were being faithful as His disciples, which is what kept them together as the church of God.

God's call is into both the Body of Christ and churches of God; they are quite distinct things. The former is perfect, seated in the heavenly places [9] in Christ (Ephesians 2:6). Nothing can spoil that relationship in any way. It is not affected by sin or disobedience. There are no conditions to remaining in it. However, the opposite is true for churches of God. They are gatherings for service and obedience. There are requirements to be met in order to be added to them, and requirements in order to remain in them. It is our human limitations and weaknesses, not God's design, that prevents us all as believers being in churches that are "churches of God." Christ is building the church which is His Body unconditionally for Himself, and it will continue in union with Him eternally. But the churches of God are a divine arrangement for the present period of time, so that God may be served acceptably in the interval until Christ returns.

Connected to the House of God

As we saw in the last section, the house of God is where God dwells on Earth among His people, who have separated themselves to Him (1 Corinthians 3:16; 2 Corinthians 6:16–18). It is the pillar and support of the truth of God (1 Timothy 3:15). It is where disciples are being built up together to worship and serve God (1 Peter 2:5,9). As we have seen in this section, the churches of God are where God intends disciples to gather to serve Him. And so Scripture closely links the house of God with the churches of God.

We see this in 1 Timothy 3:5,15 where taking care of a church of God is described as being part of the conduct expected in the house of God: *"If a man does not know how to manage his own household, how will he take care of the church of God? ... I write so that you will know how one ought to conduct himself in the household of God, which is the church of the living God, the pillar and support of the truth."*

We see it also in Ephesians 2:21,22 where the church in Ephesus is described as being part of the holy temple that God is building: *"In whom the whole building, being fitted together, is growing into a holy temple in the Lord, in whom you also are being built together into a dwelling of God in the Spirit."* In addition, we see it in the linkage of the spiritual worship of those in the house of God with their gathering themselves together in Hebrews 10:25: *"Since we have a great priest over the house of God, let us draw near with a sincere heart in full assurance of faith ... and let us consider how to stimulate one another to love and good deeds, not forsaking our own assembling together ..."*

We see it again in 1 Corinthians 3:16 where the church of God in Corinth was told: *"Do you not know that you are [a] temple of God and that the Spirit of God dwells in you?"* And so Scripture teaches that it is those disciples gathered in churches of God that form God's house on Earth today, as a collective entity.

Connected to the Kingdom of God

The kingdom of God is the community on Earth where Christ's authority is collectively acknowledged and carried out (Matthew 6:10). The kingdom was given to Israel in the past (Exodus 19:6), but they eventually lost it due to their unfaithfulness and disobedience. It was then transferred to the apostles and other disciples gathered with them, as Christ told them, *"Do not be afraid, little flock, for your Father has chosen gladly to give you the kingdom"* (Luke 12:32). Subsequently the kingdom also included others who were added to them (Acts 8:12; 14:22; 19:8), as "the flock of God" (1 Peter 5:2). It is therefore a place for disciples, believers who genuinely wish to be obedient to Him in unity. The governing law of the kingdom is "the faith", which is what the apostles taught (Acts 14:22).

It was concerning the kingdom of God that the Lord Jesus gave instructions to his apostles before his departure (Acts 1:1-6), and that caused them to establish churches of God wherever they went. It was what the apostle Paul devoted himself to: *"He stayed two full years in his own rented quarters and was welcoming all who came to him, preaching the kingdom of God and teaching concerning the Lord Jesus Christ with all openness, unhindered"* (Acts 28:30,31).

For example, when Paul and Barnabas were travelling in Asia Minor, they returned to revisit three churches—in Lystra, Iconium, and Antioch. It says that while they were there they were: *"... strengthening the souls of the disciples, encouraging them to continue in the faith, and saying, 'Through many tribulations we must enter the kingdom of God.' When they had appointed elders for them in every church, having prayed with fasting, they commended them to the Lord in whom they had believed"* (Acts 14:22,23).

Here we see the close connection between the disciples in the local churches of God, with their governing elders, adhering to the faith as the teaching of the Lord that bound them together, all in the kingdom of God.

We further see the connection between the churches and the kingdom (and priesthood) in Revelation 1:4–6: *"John to the seven churches that are in Asia ... He has made us to be a kingdom, priests to His God and Father."* And so, once again, it becomes clear that those who are gathered in churches of God constitute the kingdom of God on Earth, as one united community.

The Same People

There is a pattern therefore, not of disparate groups or entities, but of the same obedient company of people, called together by God to reflect various aspects of His work and relationships with them. All believers are made living stones, sons (and daughters) of God, and are given a birth-right to priesthood at their new birth, when they confess the Son of God as their Saviour and Lord. They have been sanctified (set apart) for those purposes.

The privileges of being the house of God, the kingdom of God, the holy and royal priesthood, the holy nation, and the people of God are spiritual realities made possible by the work of Christ. But they must be reflected on Earth by believers' obedience in accordance with God's order.

The living stones must come to be built up in conjunction with the corner stone in order to be a house for God; that is the purpose of living stones. The priests have to function together in it as the priesthood under the great high priest; priests do not just function individually. Disciples are to be joined together in a community of churches, as the kingdom of God, under God's rule. And His sons and daughters have to separate themselves to God to allow Him to regard them as His people (2 Corinthians 6:16-18). This is the divine ideal, and it should be what we as members of the Body of Christ long for also, that all living believers in Christ would constitute these entities on Earth.

Who Are Included?

The epistles were written to saints gathered together in churches of God. It is in these epistles where we are given the teaching of the house of God, the kingdom of God and other related matters, because it pertained to them. For example, it was to saints in these churches in various places, who had been baptized(1 Peter 3:21) and who were under elders (1 Peter 5:1–3), that the apostle Peter wrote that they were being built up as a spiritual house, that they were a holy priesthood and a royal priesthood (the same priesthood but in different aspects), and that they were a holy nation (1 Peter 2:5,9). He described them as having been chosen to obey Jesus Christ.

It was the faithful saints in the church at Ephesus that the apostle Paul described as having been built on the foundation of the apostles and prophets, being fitly framed together to be the temple of God, and being a habitation of God in the Spirit (Ephesians 2:20–22). It was to the saints in the church of God in Corinth that Paul wrote that they were part of the temple (house) of God, and that this required them to be separate from ungodly associations (1 Corinthians 3:16; 2 Corinthians 6:16-18). It was to those who were under overseers that the writer of Hebrews said were the house of God (Hebrews 3:6; 13:17), and that they were receiving the kingdom of God (Hebrews 12:28)[10]. Nowhere does it indicate that any believer not gathered in churches of God was in the temple, or the house, or the kingdom of God.

Important Distinctions

And so there are important connections between these various terms that we have been looking at. Three of them—all containing the expression "of God"—refer to the same people, but describe a different aspect of their relationship with Him:

- The church (and churches) of God, focusing on disciples being gathered together in particular places for service and testimony in response to the call of God.
- The house of God, focusing on God living among these people, receiving their priestly service.
- The kingdom of God, focusing on their collective subjection to the rule and authority of God, and their resulting conduct.

Aspirations or Conditions?

As we saw in chapter 1, our on-going obedience as disciples of
the Lord Jesus does not affect our membership in the church the
Body of Christ. But, as we have been discovering, this is not true
for each of these other relationships. For example:

- Churches of God: Since they are to be a testimony to
  God in each place where they are located, disciples must
  be added to them, continue in obedience as they are
  taught, and maintain their standard of holiness. Sin
  must be dealt with, and saints may have to be put away
  from them (1 Corinthians 5:11). It is even possible for
  an entire church to cease to exist for God (Revelation
  2:5).
- The house of God: Since it is to be a holy priesthood,
  drawing near and offering spiritual sacrifices, making
  confession to God's name, those in it must continue
  faithfully and sincerely to exercise the privilege of doing
  so (Hebrews 3:6). It must stand for and testify to the
  truth of God (1 Timothy 3:15).
- The kingdom of God: Since it is the place where the
  rule of God is obeyed, and His righteousness is
  exhibited, those in it must live righteous lives. The
  unrighteous are disqualified from having a part in it (1
  Corinthians 6:10; Galatians 5:21; Ephesians 5:5).

These conditions are not set forth in Scripture merely as
aspirations for those who are in the churches, the house, and the
kingdom, but rather as on-going conditions. In all these cases,
continued faithfulness is required. Willful disobedience,

ungodly living, disregard of God's truth, or refusal to take advantage of the spiritual privileges that Christ has obtained for us can cause us to forfeit or miss the privileges of these relationships during our lifetimes. Clearly these three things that are "of God" cannot be synonymous with the church that is Christ's Body.

On the other hand, God is extremely compassionate towards honest weakness and failings. We are not expected to have perfect understanding or to achieve sinlessness (1 John 1:8). Provision is made for our ignorance and failure. Nothing is expected of us that we cannot do (2 Corinthians 8:12). But willful disregard of the things of God is quite a different matter: "*God is opposed to the proud, but gives grace to the humble*" (1 Peter 5:5). It is important that we understand the distinctions between these expressions, so that we do not assume that as believers we are automatically included in all of these things. The major point, however, is that God desires that all living members of the Body of Christ in fact be part of the churches of God, the house of God, and the kingdom of God, and aim to show in practice the character of the church the Body of Christ in their lives together. That is the ideal to which we as believers in the Lord Jesus should aspire.

CHAPTER EIGHT: GOD'S CHURCH – A SUMMARY

Following is a summary of the main points that we have seen in this book as we have explored the subject of God's church and churches:

- Gathering together in churches is important for disciples. We are not intended merely to serve God alone as individuals.
- It is not left to us to choose where or how to gather. God has prescribed what His church is, and He calls disciples into it through His Word.
- Local churches in the New Testament were referred to as "churches of God." To be a church of God, a church must (a) be built on the foundation teaching of the apostles, (b) be built together in full fellowship with other churches of God, and (c) be built up in spiritual life and service.
- The churches of God are not the same as the Body of Christ, which consists of all believers in Christ from Pentecost until His return to the air. A member of that Body can never cease to be so, regardless of their spiritual condition. However, being in a church of God requires being added to it, and then staying in it.
- The first church of God in Jerusalem set a pattern for us today. It began with disciples being saved, then baptized, and then added, and then continuing in the apostles' teaching, the fellowship, the breaking of bread

and the prayers.

- As more churches came into existence, they were formed on the same basis, and they maintained a unity of teaching and practice. They continued as one community.

- Leadership in the churches was initially exercised by the apostles, then passed to other elders who were not apostles, who acted collectively. They were supported by deacons. The elders had the responsibility for the pastoral care of the saints. Unity among the entire elderhood was necessary in order to maintain the common teaching and practice of the community.

- Spiritual gifts have been given to all believers. In the local churches, they are to be used in harmony to strengthen spiritually the saints in them, as well as to make other disciples and to do good to others.

- Within the churches there are distinct roles for men and women, and God's order puts some restrictions on the activities of women.

- Godly living and faithful service is expected of saints in churches of God. Sin by someone in a church taints the church and must be dealt with even, where necessary, to the extent of putting the person away. The eventual aim of such discipline, however, is their subsequent restoration.

---

[1] In those early days, baptism was also a public declaration by Jewish believers of their allegiance to Jesus the Messiah, whom their nation had just rejected and crucified. They were setting themselves apart from what their

leaders had done. When the gospel began being proclaimed to Gentiles, we see the current order: receiving the Holy Spirit at salvation, with baptism by immersion to follow (Acts 10:44-48).

[2] The error of "baptismal regeneration"—that a person must be baptized in water to be eternally saved—is what led to the baptism of newborn infants in the centuries following the New Testament. This was eventually changed to sprinkling for safety reasons (and eventually led to the use of "holy water").

[3] This is one of the differences between a church of God and the church the Body of Christ.

[4] Matthias had been with the Lord (Acts 1:21-23). Paul was given a special revelation by the Lord to equip him for his work (Acts 26:16-18; 1 Corinthians 9:1; 11:23; 15:8).

[5] This reference to the laying on of hands by the elders together in 1 Timothy 4:14 was for the purpose of jointly recognizing Timothy's gift and commending him to his sphere of service. The word used for "by" is "*meta*"—meaning that it was "accompanied by" the laying on of hands, not "by means of." This act did not confer any special powers, such as had been the case in Acts 8:18, where the word "*dia*" is used, indicating "by means of."

[6] Examples of such joint action are: (a) the commendation of Timothy, a brother to accompany Paul, by the brethren of two assemblies (Acts 16:2), who may well have constituted (or been part of) the "presbytery" (group of elders) who publicly recognized his gift and ministry; and (b) the joint appointment by churches of a brother to travel with the apostle Paul and Titus in their work of delivering a gift from the saints (2 Corinthians 8:18-20).

[7] This has nothing to do with inherent superiority or inferiority, but with God's prescribed order.

[8] This church situation is distinct from a marriage relationship, for example, where there are also distinct roles of headship and subjection between husbands and wives, which Paul deals with in Ephesians 5:22–33.

[9] "The heavenlies" (Greek: *'epouranios'*) (Ephesians 1:3, 20; 2:6; 3:10; 6:12) is to be distinguished from "the holy place" in the immediate presence of God (Hebrews 9:8, 12, 24; 10:19), which is discussed in chapter 6 and elsewhere.

[10] Those in the church in Corinth were also told that they were members of the Body of Christ (1 Corinthians 12:27); but they were also told that this was due to them having been baptized in the Holy Spirit (1 Corinthians 12:13) and so it applies to all who come in faith to Christ.

Did you love *Discovering God's Church*? Then you should read
The Eternal Purpose: God's Master Plan for the Ages[1] by Keith
Dorricott!

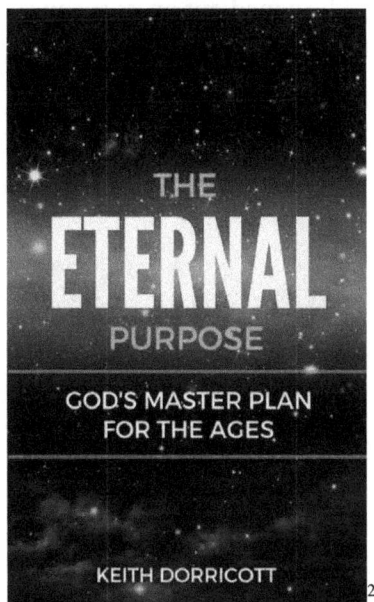

In this book, Keith Dorricott spans the whole range of human
history and beyond to outline God's exciting and eternal
purpose and explain how God has, and will, achieve it through
six distinct ages, also known as dispensations:Chapter 1:The
Purpose of the AgesChapter 2:The Age of ConscienceChapter 3:
The Age of Human RuleChapter 4: The Age of PromiseChapter
5: The Age of the LawChapter 6: The Age of GraceChapter
7: The Ages to ComeAs part of the exposition, God's special

---

1. https://books2read.com/u/mqpnGO

2. https://books2read.com/u/mqpnGO

relationship with his special people, Israel is traced, including God's relationship with key patriarchal figures such as Adam, Noah, Abraham, Isaac and Jacob, together with a look at what the future has in store for the nation of Israel (and how God will not allow it to be wiped out by its enemies) and the Gentile nations, as revealed in Bible prophecy.

Also by Keith Dorricott

The Eternal Purpose: God's Master Plan for the Ages
Our Spiritual Journey
Christian Counseling - How to Help Yourself and Others Live
Biblically
Tracing Our Roots - The History of the Churches of God From
Pentecost to Today
Uncovering the Pattern: God's Way of Unity For Disciples
Today
I Want to Live: The Story of My Battle with Leukemia, My
Journey of Discovery, and the Many Who Helped in My
Healing
Discovering God's Church
Discovering God's House
Discovering True Worship

www.ingramcontent.com/pod-product-compliance
Lightning Source LLC
Chambersburg PA
CBHW071927020426
42331CB00010B/2752